CONTENTS

ABOUT THE AUTHOR

Celtic Heritage Magazine said of **Roger Landes**: "Not only is Landes helping to legitimize the instrument—he is taking it to a whole other level." Roger took up the bouzouki in 1981, cofounding the popular Celtic band Scartaglen. A first-rate accompanist, he is also known for exploring the playing of traditional Irish melodies on the bouzouki. His critically acclaimed recording *Dragon Reels* showcased the instrument's melodic capabilities. Roger is the founder and artistic director of ZoukFest World Music Camp in Santa Fe, New Mexico. He has appeared on the National Public Radio shows *Mountain Stage* and *A Prairie Home Companion*, and his music was featured in the PBS documentary *Last Stand of the Tallgrass Prairie*.

INTRODUCTION

The Irish bouzouki is an extremely versatile instrument that is a great deal of fun to play. You can use it to accompany dance tunes in a Celtic band or session, accompany your own voice, or play the melodies yourself! The Irish bouzouki seems to combine attributes of both the mandolin and guitar, while some are intrigued by its Middle Eastern roots. Still others hear in it the droning strains of the Appalachian mountain dulcimer. But the vast majority of people who play the Irish bouzouki are drawn to it by its use in Irish folk and traditional music, and that will be our focus here in the *Hal Leonard Irish Bouzouki Method*. The bouzouki is most often used for accompaniment, and that's where we will start.

ABOUT THE AUDIO

To access the audio examples that accompany this book, simply go to **www.halleonard.com/mylibrary** and enter the code found on page 1. The examples that include audio demonstration tracks are marked with an icon throughout the book. The bouzouki accompaniment part will be in your stereo's left channel, while the melody (on tenor banjo or mandolin) will be in the right channel. Use your balance control to isolate each part. You may find it particularly helpful to listen to the left (accompaniment) channel while you are learning the parts, then listen to the right (melody) channel to practice them. By all means, learn the melodies, too, if you are interested. They are notated along with the accompaniment parts.

THE IRISH BOUZOUKI

Related to the family of instruments descending from the ancient Mesopotamian *tanbur*, the Irish bouzouki is a recent hybrid resulting from the introduction of the round-backed Greek bouzouki into Irish traditional music in the late 1960s. Early Irish bouzouki pioneers include Johnny Moynihan (Sweeney's Men, Planxty), Andy Irvine (Sweeney's Men, Planxty), Dónal Lunny (Planxty, The Bothy Band), and Alec Finn (De Dannan). All four experimented with the Greek bouzouki before acquiring flat-backed "Irish" bouzoukis (with the exception of Alec Finn, who still plays a Greek bouzouki). Used almost exclusively for accompanying dance tunes and songs, the Irish bouzouki quickly caught on, and today it is ensconced in traditional music-making in Ireland as well as in Irish music-playing communities around the globe. As for whether it is here to stay, only time will tell.

Greek bouzouki

Irish bouzouki

HOW TO FIND AN IRISH BOUZOUKI

The finest Irish bouzoukis are obtained directly from the people who build them, but there are several inexpensive factory-made examples available from music retailers.

BEFORE YOU PURCHASE

Chances are you already have an instrument before buying this book, but if not, it is a really good idea to get your hands on one to try out before you purchase, preferably in the company of someone else who plays. Attending a music festival or camp can also expose one to a variety of instruments. An internet search for "Irish Festival" should yield a plethora of choices during the summer festival season.

IRISH BOUZOUKI ANATOMY

Because it is still developing, the Irish bouzouki does not have a standardized design as do other, more common fretted instruments like the steel-string guitar or the mandolin. Even after 40 years of development (the first Irish bouzouki was built in 1970), designs for the instrument still vary widely from builder to builder. Most have pear-shaped bodies with flat tops and backs, four **courses**, or pairs, of strings, and long, slender necks with 24- to 26-inch (61–66cm) scale length. Shorter-scaled versions, often called "octave mandolins," exist, as well as those with carved, arched tops and backs. Some have five courses of strings (in which case many insist on calling them *citterns*). Others have only three courses. The long-scale, four-course, flat-top/flat-back design is by far the most prevalent.

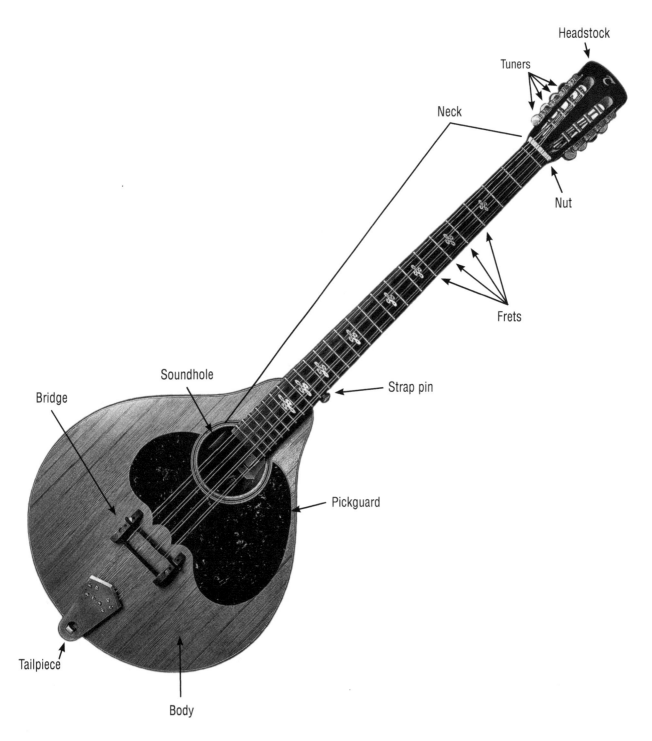

Irish bouzouki by Herb Taylor, Golden, CO (2011)

PLAYING POSITION

Seated

Standing

Irish bouzouki by Herb Taylor, Golden, CO (2010)

THE STRAP

Notice that in both seated and standing positions the player is using a strap. Because of the shape of the bouzouki, using a strap is very helpful to maintain good posture and free both hands up for playing instead of holding the instrument.

POSTURE

Notice also that the player's back is nice and straight and that he is not twisting at the waist. His arms hang comfortably from his shoulders—he is not holding them up. His wrists are straight and his left-hand fingers are nicely curled with his fingertips always pointing towards the strings.

The bouzouki neck is roughly 45 degrees up from horizontal and about 30 degrees out from the player's chest. This facilitates good fret-hand position.

When standing, there is no way to avoid damping the back of the instrument, but since many players only stand when performing, they are often using a sound system, and that will offset the loss of volume caused by damping the back with the chest/belly. I stand when I have to, but I greatly prefer to sit when I play. I believe I can put much more of my energy into the music when seated.

The neck angles when seated can be maintained when standing by carefully positioning the instrument. Notice how the instrument will now pivot on the strap. Lift the neck to 45 degrees from horizontal. See that the neck is also tilting out away from the chest, making room for the left arm.

THE PICK HAND

POSITION

The pick hand (the right hand for right-handed folks) should be positioned over the strings just in front of the bridge. It is common to touch the strings behind the bridge very lightly with the lower palm of the hand as a guide more than anything else. Do not plant the hand on the strings—it will damp the sound and inhibit good picking technique.

HOLDING THE PICK

There are many different types of picks (or *plectrums*) available, and while tastes vary, what seems to work best is a medium thickness pick. (I prefer the Clayton Acetal Polymer large triangle size in .063mm.) To hold the pick, imagine that it has a vertical line running through the center of it. Place the pick between thumb and index finger so that the vertical line is perpendicular to the thumb. Make sure to curl the index finger behind the pick to keep it out of the way of the point of the pick. Keep the thumb straight and relaxed—do not bend the thumb in order to hold the pick.

THE FRET HAND

Depending on the width and thickness of your bouzouki's neck, you may wish to use either a guitar-style fret-hand position, with the thumb on the back of the neck (particularly if your neck is wide, and flat on the back)…

…or a mandolin-style hand position, with the neck perched between the second joint of the thumb and the first joint of the index finger (particularly if your neck is narrow, and/or with a "V"-shaped back).

THE THUMB

Regardless of which hand position works better for your neck, the thumb needs to be relaxed. Do not fall into the habit of holding the neck in a vise-like "death grip."

TUNING YOUR BOUZOUKI

The audio accompanying this book includes a set of tones to which you can tune your bouzouki by ear. We start with the first course—the highest, D. Match both of the strings in your instrument's first course to this recorded note by plucking each individual string and slowly turning the tuners on the bouzouki's headstock. Repeat with the second course, A, then the third course, D, and finally the fourth course, G.

high	1st course	=	D
↑	2nd course	=	A
↓	3rd course	=	D
low	4th course	=	G

ELECTRONIC TUNERS

Electronic tuners can be very handy; most are very accurate and allow players to get into tune very quickly. They are also really helpful for tuning in a noisy environment, in a pub session, or on stage, where you cannot control the amount of noise others are making.

MUSIC NOTATION

Reading music notation is an indispensable skill, particularly for the professional musician. Many traditional Irish musicians never learn to read notation; their customary way of learning is by listening and observation. Written music is usually not a part of this process, and it is difficult to accurately notate the way the music is really played. Because of this, the musical portions of this book are written in both standard notation and **tablature**.

Music is written (notated) on a **staff**. The staff has five lines and four spaces. The location of the note on the staff determines its pitch (highness or lowness). The higher on the staff the note is written, the higher it sounds (and vice versa).

STAFF

At the beginning of the staff is a **clef sign**. The clef sign indicating notes for the bouzouki is called the **treble clef**.

TREBLE CLEF

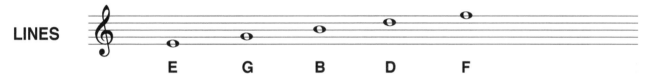

Each line and space of the staff has a letter name. The lines are from bottom to top: E G B D F (**E**very **G**ood **B**oy **D**oes **F**ine).

LINES

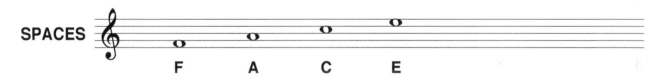

E G B D F

The spaces from bottom to top are: F A C E (**FACE**).

SPACES

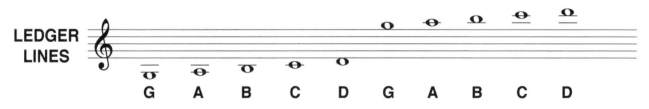

F A C E

Notes are written above and below the staff with lines called **ledger lines**.

LEDGER LINES

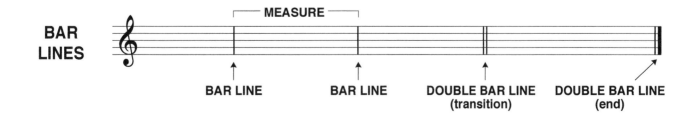

G A B C D G A B C D

Once you've determined the pitch of the notes, then a **rhythm** or time value must be established. In music, time is determined by a beat (or pulse). Beats are grouped together into **bars** (or **measures**) by **bar lines**. A **double bar** is used to show that a transition is approaching, or that it is the end of the piece.

BAR LINES

MEASURE

BAR LINE   BAR LINE   DOUBLE BAR LINE (transition)   DOUBLE BAR LINE (end)

TABLATURE

Tablature (or "tab") is an ancient method of notating music for fretted instruments. In tab, the strings of the instrument are represented by horizontal lines. The frets are shown by numbers written on those lines.

The tab represents the strings of the instrument. The lowest course (G) is represented by the bottom tab line, and the highest course (D) is shown as the top line.

Numbers on the tab lines represent the fret at which your left fingers press the strings. A zero means that the string is played open or unfretted.

In this example, three single notes on three different strings are played in succession. The first string (D) is played open, the second string (A) is played at the third fret, and the fourth string (G) is played at the fifth fret.

Playing two or more notes simultaneously—called a **chord** —is indicated in tab with stacked notes.

TIME SIGNATURES

The **time signature**, or **meter**, shows two things: the number on top shows us the number of beats in a measure (it is also the number we will count to), and the number on the bottom shows us what type of note gets one of those beats. You'll learn more about the different types of notes shortly.

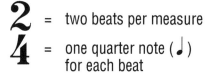

4 = four beats per measure
4 = one quarter note (♩) for each beat

2 = two beats per measure
4 = one quarter note (♩) for each beat

OPEN STRINGS

The open strings of the Irish bouzouki are tuned (low to high) **G D A D**.

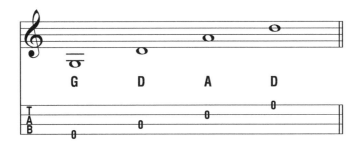

PICKING

This sign signifies striking the strings with a **downstroke** (⊓), with the hand moving the pick down toward the floor.

This sign signifies an **upstroke** (∨), with the hand moving upward toward the ceiling.

Play the study below along with the audio track using all downstrokes. At the start of the track, you'll hear four clicks before the playing begins that establish the **tempo**, or speed, of the exercise. Each click represents one beat. This exercise is played in all **quarter notes** (one note per beat in 4/4 time). It helps to tap your foot and count "1-2-3-4" on each beat.

🔊 OPEN-STRING STUDY

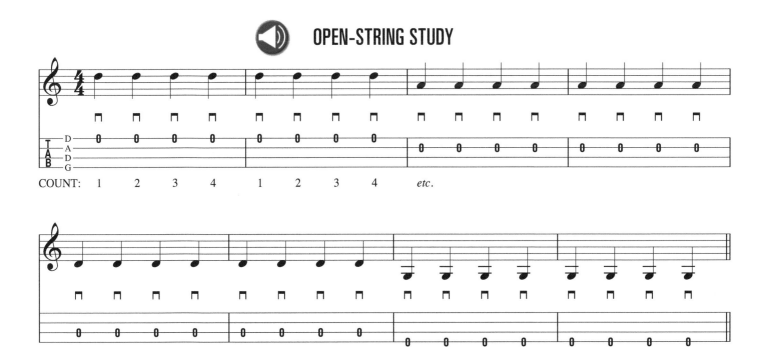

DOWN-UP PICKING

The simplest picking pattern is the **down-up picking** pattern, an alternating pattern of downstrokes and upstrokes with the pick hand. This is the basic pattern for the reels, hornpipes, and polkas we will be playing later in this book.

Be sure to play each note at the same volume in this exercise.

Play along with the accompanying audio track. Make sure you match the rhythm on the recording.

🔊 DOWN-UP PICKING 1

EIGHTH NOTES

Eighth notes represent a quarter note split into two equal parts:

Eighth notes are often coupled, or **beamed** together. When four are used in a sequence, they are usually all beamed together as well.

One quarter note equals two eighth notes beamed together:

When you play the two eighth notes in sequence, the first note is played when your foot taps down, and the second is played when your foot raises up. The two eighth notes represent one beat. You count two eighth notes as "1 and."

Now we play the down-up picking exercise in eighth notes. Again, be careful to play each note at the same volume and follow the tempo of the clicks.

🔊 DOWN-UP PICKING 2

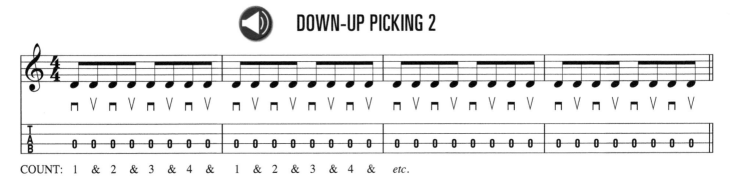

COUNT: 1 & 2 & 3 & 4 &   1 & 2 & 3 & 4 &   *etc.*

SIXTEENTH NOTES

Sixteenth notes represent a quarter note split into four equal parts:

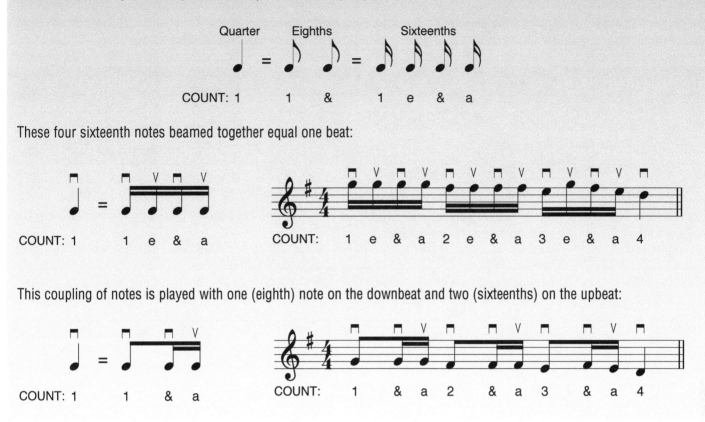

These four sixteenth notes beamed together equal one beat:

This coupling of notes is played with one (eighth) note on the downbeat and two (sixteenths) on the upbeat:

Next we will play the down-up picking exercise in sixteenth notes. Play each note at the same volume and make sure you match the rhythm on the recording. It helps to count "1-ee-and-ah, 2-ee-and-ah," etc., when playing sixteenth notes.

🔊 DOWN-UP PICKING 3

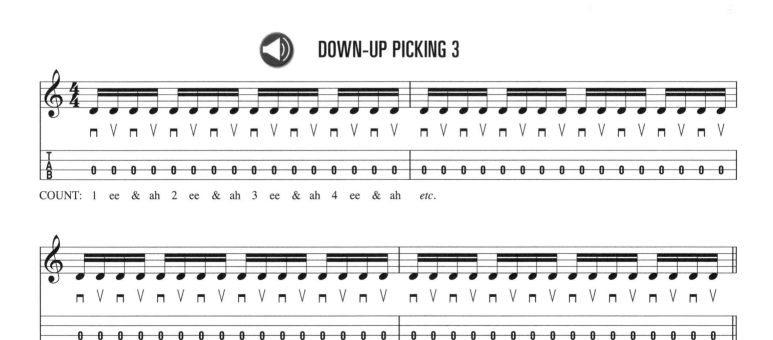

COUNT: 1 ee & ah 2 ee & ah 3 ee & ah 4 ee & ah *etc.*

DOWN-UP-DOWN PICKING

Irish music has a few "unusual" rhythms—**double jig**, **single jig**, **slide**, **slip jig**, and **hop jig**—that are different from those used in most American music. They require a different picking pattern called **down-up-down picking**.

6/8 TIME AND JIGS

The exercise below is in a 6/8 time signature, the same meter as a double jig.

Rather than counting "1, 2, 3, 4, 5, 6," jigs are counted "one-and-uh, two-and-uh." In 6/8 time, the **dotted quarter note** (♩.) takes up three beats, the length of "one-and-uh."

Play this exercise along with the accompanying audio track. Notice that you are playing the **downbeats**, matching the clicks. Again, strive to play each note at the same volume.

🔊 DOWN-UP-DOWN PICKING 1

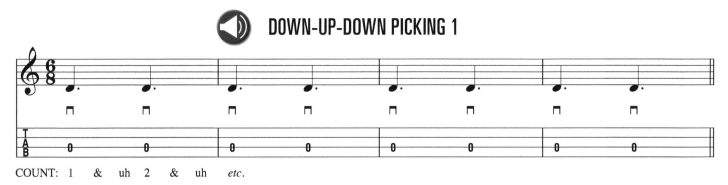

COUNT: 1 & uh 2 & uh *etc.*

Now we'll add another note to the exercise. Notice that you are playing the downbeats, matching the clicks, but you are also playing another note that comes just before the downbeats. When counting along, this extra note is played when you say "uh."

🔊 DOWN-UP-DOWN PICKING 2

COUNT: 1 & uh 2 & uh *etc.*

Next we'll add an upstroke between the first and third notes on every beat, still playing on the open third course. The picking pattern now is "down-up-down." Make sure you are playing the picking pattern only as written. This is very important!

Play the exercise along with the audio track. Notice that now you are playing all three notes on every downbeat (six eighth notes per measure). Again, be careful to play each note at the same volume.

🔊 DOWN-UP-DOWN PICKING 3

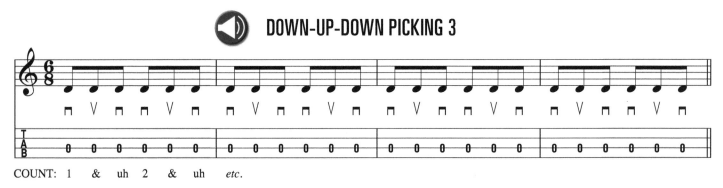

COUNT: 1 & uh 2 & uh *etc.*

Now play the exercise below. This one includes larger jumps between notes than the last. Be sure to keep the down-up-down pattern going throughout.

DOWN-UP-DOWN PICKING 5

CROSSING STRINGS

Now you are ready for an exercise that involves **string crossing**. This is very important on the Irish bouzouki because picking across the strings—as opposed to simply strumming across them—is the key to the characteristic accompaniment textures used by the great Irish players. Play the exercise, taking your time and making sure to maintain the down-up-down pattern throughout. Make sure you do not change this picking pattern when picking different strings.

REPEATS

The **repeat signs** ‖: :‖ show that the music in between them should be repeated in one continuous flow. In the following example, when you reach the repeat sign at the end of the first passage, immediately return to the first sign and play the passage again. Then proceed to the next passage, and follow the repeat signs there too.

A pair of repeat signs usually means you play the music twice, unless you see a special instruction over the staff like "Play 3 times."

DOWN-UP-DOWN PICKING 6

Now we'll take this further by playing an exercise with a more contiguous melody. Take it slowly, and make sure you maintain the down-up-down picking pattern throughout.

DOWN-UP-DOWN PICKING 7

KEY SIGNATURES AND ENDINGS

If a tune is in a key with one or more sharp or flat notes, we add a **key signature** at the beginning. This key signature indicates that every F note in the music should be played as F#:

Sometimes a melody is repeated, but does not end in exactly the same way the second time around. That's why we use first and second **endings** to distinguish between two variations of a melody.

When you reach the repeat sign, return to the beginning and play the part again. On the second time through the part, skip over the first ending (the bracketed measure labeled with a "1"), go to the second ending, and continue from there.

FIRST TUNE:
THE KINNEGAD SLASHERS

"The Kinnegad Slashers" is in the key of D (as indicated by the key signature). It includes a **pickup** and first and second endings. A pickup is an introductory phrase of one or more notes that comes before the first beat of the first measure. This tune begins with an eighth-note pickup that you can play as an upstroke. Listen to the audio to hear how this sounds.

The melody, usually played by a mandolin or other higher-range instrument, is written and recorded here for your reference. At the typical Irish session, melodies are rarely played on bouzouki, but a good accompanist needs to know the whole tune. Listen, read along, and get familiar with it, then learn the following accompaniment parts. Later, if you are up for a good challenge, you can come back and learn the melody.

THE KINNEGAD SLASHERS — MELODY

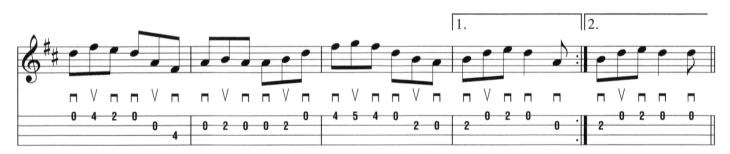

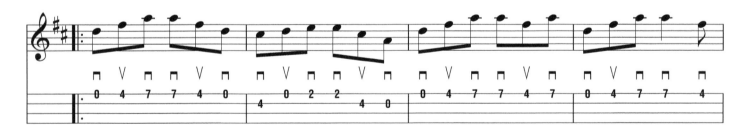

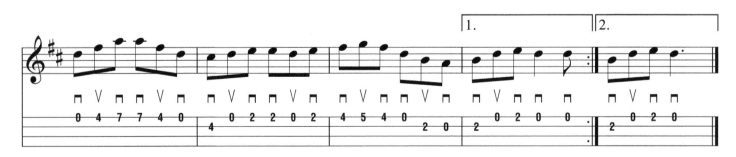

THE KINNEGAD SLASHERS DRONE ACCOMPANIMENT

A **drone** is simply a single sustained or repeated note that is the same as the **tonic** note, or bottom note of the key. If a tune is in D major, then the tonic is D.

Practice playing a drone to accompany "The Kinnegad Slashers." Start with only the open third course. Begin by playing the dotted quarter notes on each downbeat, using only downstrokes.

THE KINNEGAD SLASHERS – DRONE 1

Play 8 times

The 5th note of the D major scale may also be combined with the tonic for an "open 5ths" drone sound. In the key of D, the 5th is A.

Now play the open second course along with the third course. Try to hear how the A in the drone increases the complexity of the harmony created with the tune, in spite of the fact that the two notes in the drone never vary. In this case the melody is providing the harmonic change.

THE KINNEGAD SLASHERS – DRONE 2

Play 8 times

Now play the first and second courses along with the third course. This gives us not only the interval of an open 5th, but now we have the **octave** of the tonic note above it (same pitch, but eight scale tones higher). Try to hear how the higher D, along with the A and the lower D, increases the complexity of the harmony created with the tune, even though the three notes in the drone never vary. Just as in the previous exercise, the melody is providing the harmonic change.

THE KINNEGAD SLASHERS – DRONE 3

Play 8 times

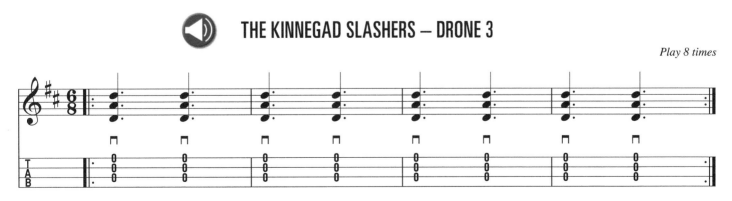

We'll stick with the same drone notes as on the previous example, but this time we'll vary them by playing a string-jumping eighth-note picking pattern with the pick hand. After playing the first course, be sure to bring your hand back up above the third course to prepare for the next downbeat. Let all three courses ring until they are picked again.

THE KINNEGAD SLASHERS – DRONE 4

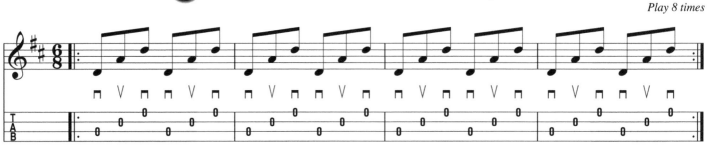

THE KINNEGAD SLASHERS RHYTHMIC DRONE ACCOMPANIMENT

Now we add more of a rhythmic "shuffling" element to the drone. Play these accompaniment exercises with all down-strokes, first on the open third course, then adding the 5th and the octave.

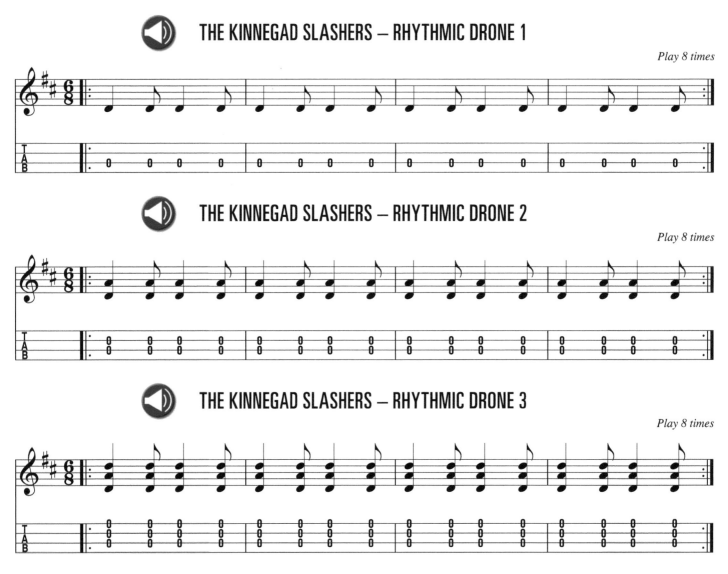

Now we add more picking to the drone. Play the open third course in a down-up-down picking pattern.

THE KINNEGAD SLASHERS — RHYTHMIC DRONE 4

Play 8 times

Adding the 5th, play both strings at once in a down-up-down pattern. Be sure to play each set of eighth notes with equal volume, playing both strings with one strum of the pick.

THE KINNEGAD SLASHERS — RHYTHMIC DRONE 5

Play 8 times

Adding the octave, keep strumming evenly, playing each beat with equal volume.

THE KINNEGAD SLASHERS — RHYTHMIC DRONE 6

Play 8 times

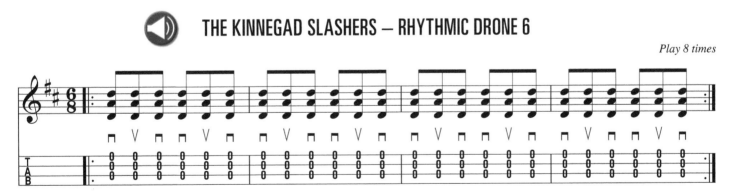

THE KINNEGAD SLASHERS CHORDS

A **chord** is defined as a group of notes that are played together at the same time. We've already been playing basic "root-5th" chords, consisting of a tonic note and a 5th.

We will continue with "root-5th" chords for more accompaniment patterns to "The Kinnegad Slashers." As in the previous exercises, we'll use just the first, second, and third courses (leaving the lowest course, G, alone for now). The D5 and A5 chords are labeled above the staff whenever a new chord or a chord change appears. (Notice that the chords don't change very often.)

Play these chords on the two downbeats in each measure. Count:

"**One** (and) (uh), **Two** (and) (uh)."

Be sure to let all three of the courses ring until you play the next chord.

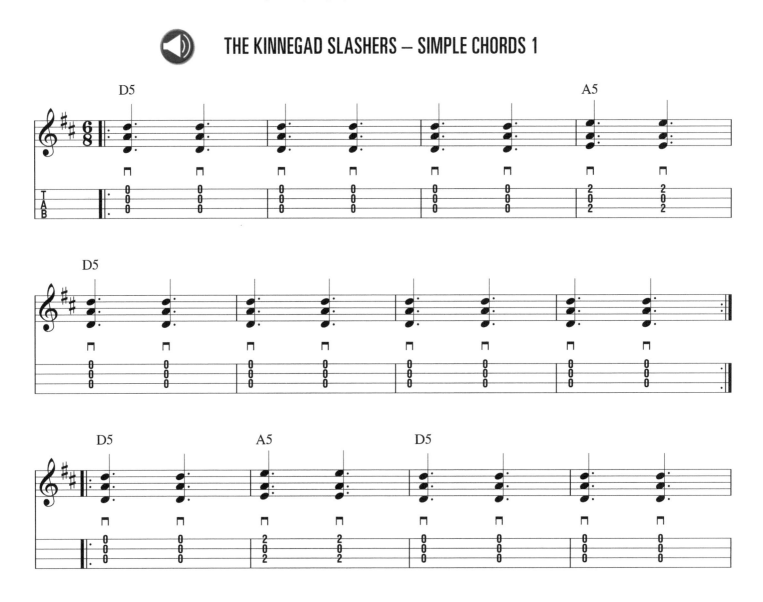

THE KINNEGAD SLASHERS – SIMPLE CHORDS 1

THE KINNEGAD SLASHERS COUNTERPOINT

When one melody is added to another and they blend in a musical way, **counterpoint** happens. This is a big part of accompaniment in Irish music. Here, the second melody functions as a melodic bass line that "walks" underneath the main melody.

THE KINNEGAD SLASHERS – SIMPLE COUNTERPOINT 1

THE KINNEGAD SLASHERS COUNTERPOINT WITH CHORDS

Now we combine simple counterpoint and basic chords. The chords change according to the tune, and the "walking" notes at the bottom add more momentum to the piece. Keep strumming on the downbeats and counting "**One**-(and)-(uh), **Two**-(and)-(uh)."

THE KINNEGAD SLASHERS – SIMPLE CHORDS 2

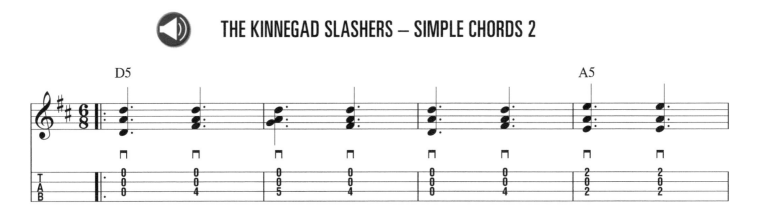

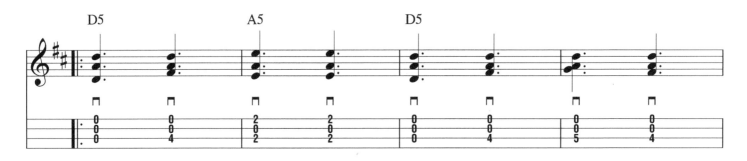

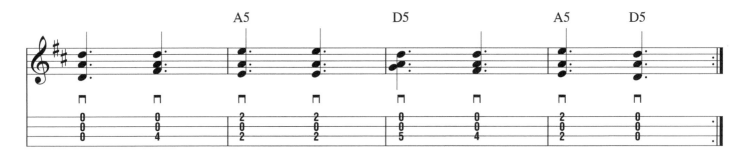

THE KINNEGAD SLASHERS COUNTERPOINT AND RHYTHMIC CHORDS

The same rhythmic patterns we explored with a rhythmic drone can be used along with counterpoint and chord changes. Play with all downstrokes.

THE KINNEGAD SLASHERS – SIMPLE COUNTERPOINT 2

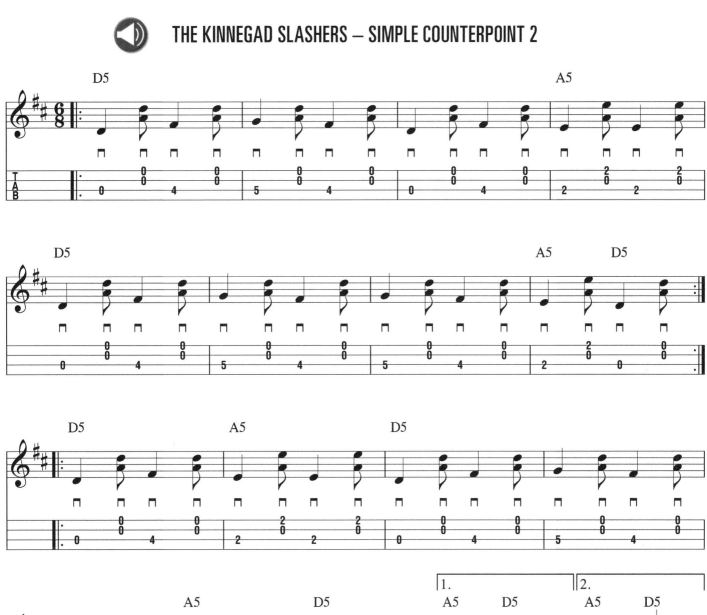

THE KINNEGAD SLASHERS COUNTERPOINT AND ARPEGGIOS

An **arpeggio** is a chord played one note at a time, often from the lowest to the highest note. We already explored simple arpeggios in the rhythmic drone section; now we combine them with chord movement and simple counterpoint. Follow the down-up-down picking pattern, and count: "**One**-(and)-(uh), **Two**-(and)-(uh)."

 THE KINNEGAD SLASHERS — SIMPLE COUNTERPOINT 3

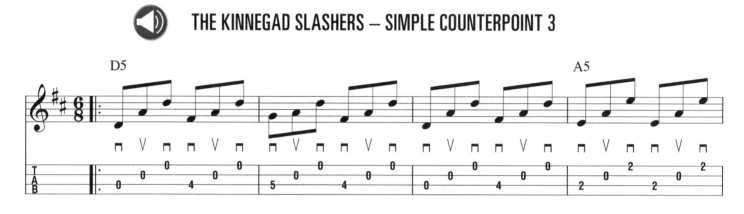

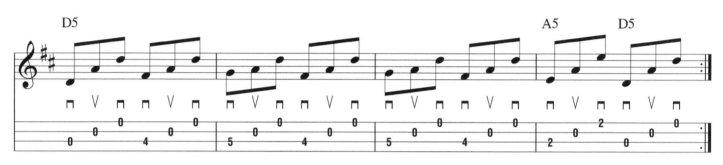

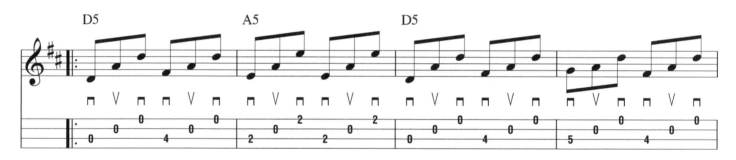

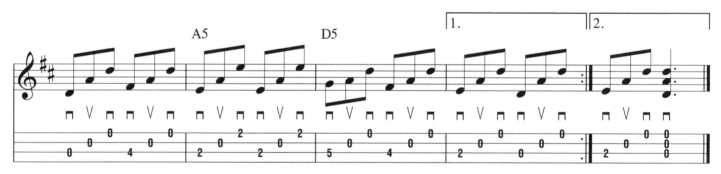

Finally, to get an idea of how "The Kinnegad Slashers" would be played at a more typical tempo for Irish session playing, listen to the next audio track. Variations of the melody and accompaniment are also typical of session playing.

 THE KINNEGAD SLASHERS — AT TEMPO

SECOND TUNE: THE SUNNY BANKS

REELS

While jigs are associated with 6/8 time, a **reel** is usually written in 2/2 or "cut" time. In cut time, which is often represented as ¢, there are two beats per measure and the **half note** gets one beat. (A half note lasts twice as long as a quarter note, and has an open notehead—see the last measure of the following tune.) As with double jigs, the pulse is two in cut time, but instead of three notes on every beat there are four.

We count reels like this:

"**One**   ee   and   uh,   **Two**   ee   and   uh."
   1   2

Our second tune, a popular reel called "The Sunny Banks," is a typical Irish **single reel**, that is, a reel with four-measure parts rather than eight-measure parts. (The fourth tune, "The Dunmore Lasses," is an example of the more common reel with eight-measure parts.) Due to their shorter parts, single reels are easy to learn and a lot of fun to play.

Listen, read along, and get familiar with this melody; then learn the following accompaniment parts.

🔊 THE SUNNY BANKS – MELODY

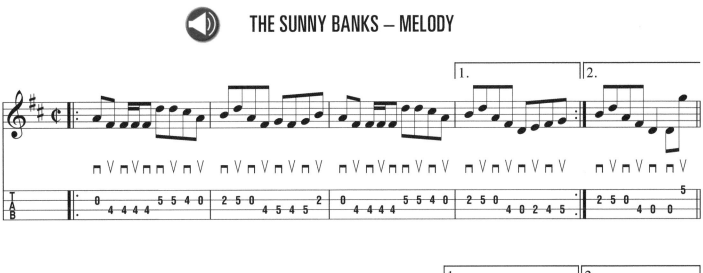

THE SUNNY BANKS DRONE ACCOMPANIMENT

As with "The Kinnegad Slashers," the drone and rhythmic drone approaches work well with this tune. We begin with a third-course drone in half notes:

THE SUNNY BANKS — DRONE 1

Now play the single-note drone in quarter notes…

THE SUNNY BANKS — DRONE 2

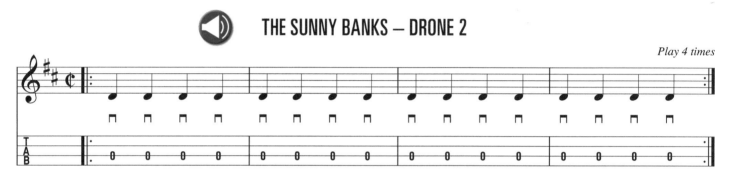

…and in eighth notes—a good exercise for quick down-up picking.

THE SUNNY BANKS — DRONE 3

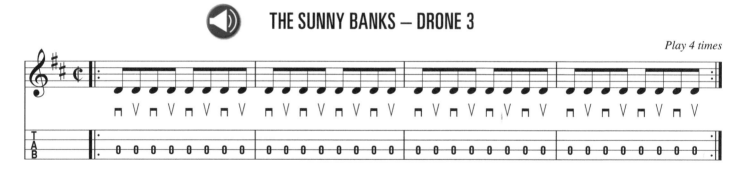

THE SUNNY BANKS RHYTHMIC DRONE ACCOMPANIMENT

Play this accompaniment with open 5ths using all downstrokes.

THE SUNNY BANKS — RHYTHMIC DRONE 1

THE SUNNY BANKS RHYTHMIC DRONE WITH ARPEGGIOS

Here it is with simple arpeggios of the open D chord. Note that you are arpeggiating up and down the chord in a four-note pattern. Use down-up picking throughout.

 THE SUNNY BANKS – RHYTHMIC DRONE 2

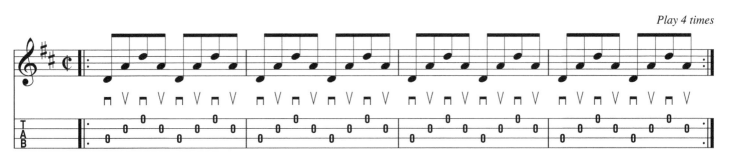

THE SUNNY BANKS CHORDS

These are basic block chords that constitute a very simple accompaniment. Now the fourth course (G) is involved, and the G chord is introduced. The thicker-sounding chords here are still based on open 5ths, but notice how the G chord contains the 3rd, B, making it a G major chord with a tonic (or **root**), 3rd, and 5th.

Also notice that the lowest note of the D chord is not the tonic—it is an A rather than D. This is called an **inversion**, and it helps to add thickness to the chord.

Note: sustaining chords played only on the downbeats, as in this example, are not the norm in Irish music, but this is a good way to get familiar with the tune's chords.

 THE SUNNY BANKS – SIMPLE CHORDS 1

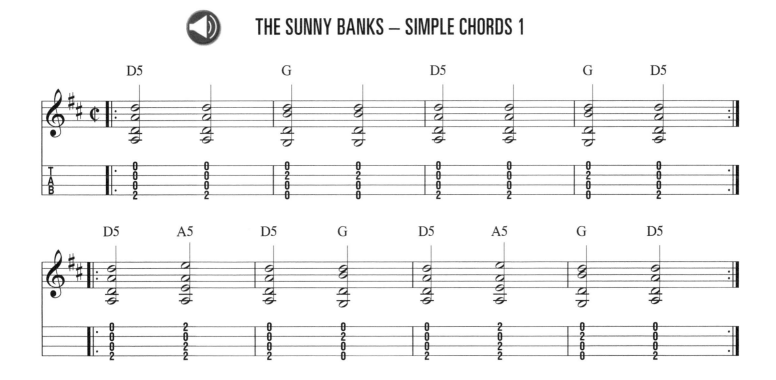

THE SUNNY BANKS RHYTHMIC CHORDS

This time the chords are broken to provide a little more rhythm. This rhythmic texture, sometimes referred to as "boom-chick," is often heard on the piano and sometimes on the guitar.

THE SUNNY BANKS — SIMPLE CHORDS 2

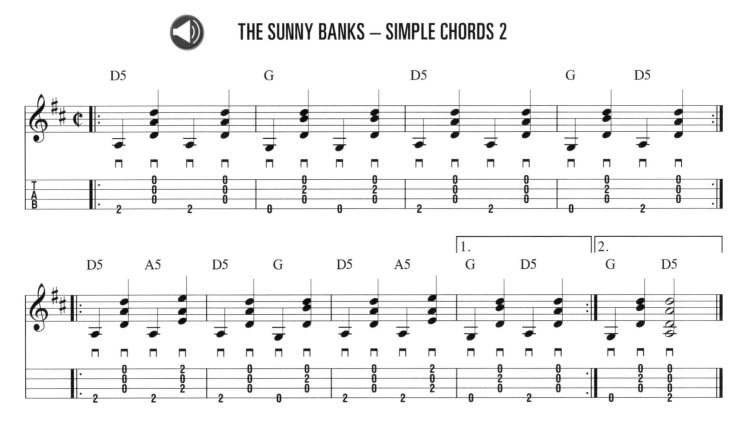

In this example, the rhythmic texture is mirroring the running eighth notes of the melody. This sort of strummed texture is often heard on the guitar but sometimes on the bouzouki.

THE SUNNY BANKS — SIMPLE CHORDS 3

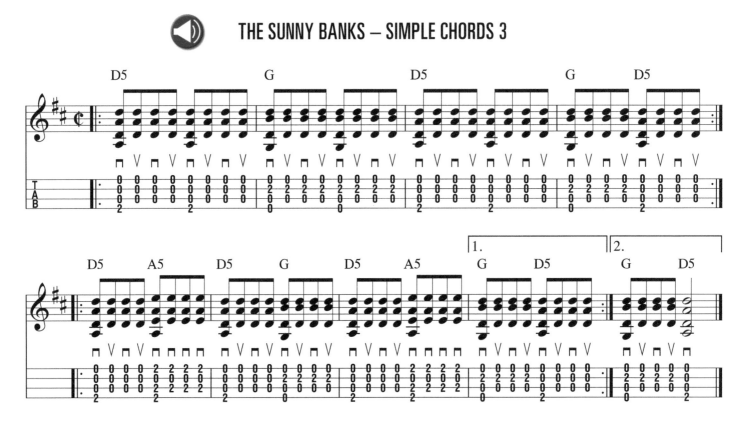

THE SUNNY BANKS COUNTERPOINT

This simple counterpoint moves under the melody line and harmonizes with the melody notes as well as the sustained open-string notes. In the second section, pick the open first and second courses while playing the counterpoint along the third course. The resulting harmony is basically D major, but still implies a chord progression via the moving notes of the counterpoint.

 THE SUNNY BANKS – COUNTERPOINT 1

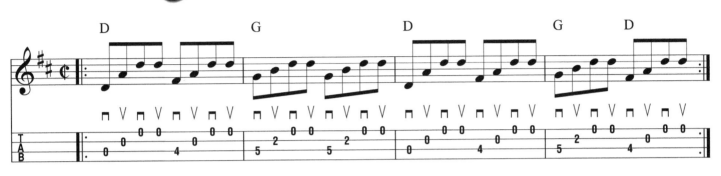

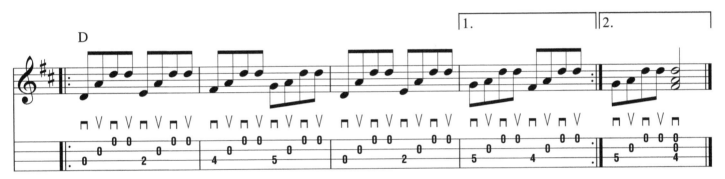

SLURS, HAMMER-ONS, AND PULL-OFFS

A curved line that connects two notes of different pitches is called a **slur**. If the second of two slurred notes is higher than the first, a **hammer-on** is called for. Pluck the first note normally, and "hammer" your finger on the second note without picking.

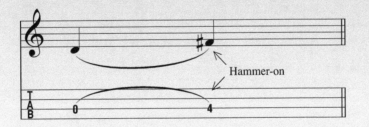

If the second of two slurred notes is lower than the first, pluck the first note and **pull off** your finger without picking.

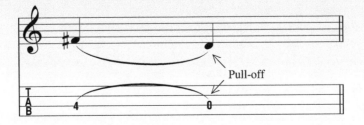

35

This counterpoint example has more fretted notes and movement providing a slightly denser harmonic texture beneath the melody. The hammer-ons contribute to the rolling rhythm. Note the surprise Asus4 chord in the fourth measure. It is essentially an A chord, but the open-string drone adds a 4th.

THE SUNNY BANKS – COUNTERPOINT 2

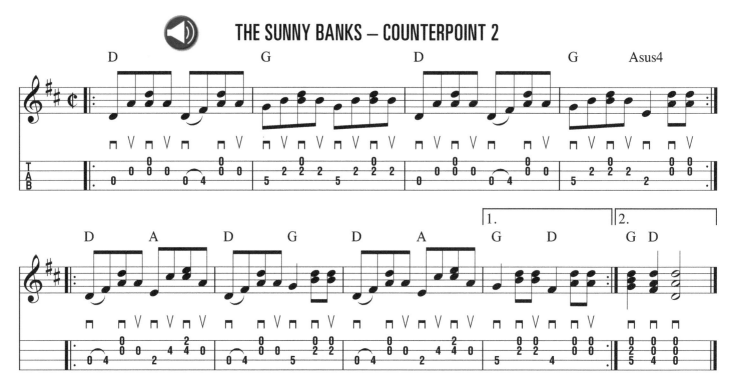

THE SUNNY BANKS RHYTHMIC COUNTERPOINT

This example has even more movement and harmony notes to the melody, and the counterpoint suggests more chords than just the D, G, and A of the previous accompaniment exercises. This is an example of the sort of rhythmic counterpoint that the best accompanists in Irish traditional music often use. Notice also that there are some **dissonances** (notes at very close intervals) that are an inevitable part of playing in this style, where there is almost always an open string ringing no matter what fretted notes you might be playing. Think of these open notes as part of the background drone that is so much a part of this music, rather than part of the chord harmony you are playing.

THE SUNNY BANKS – COUNTERPOINT 3

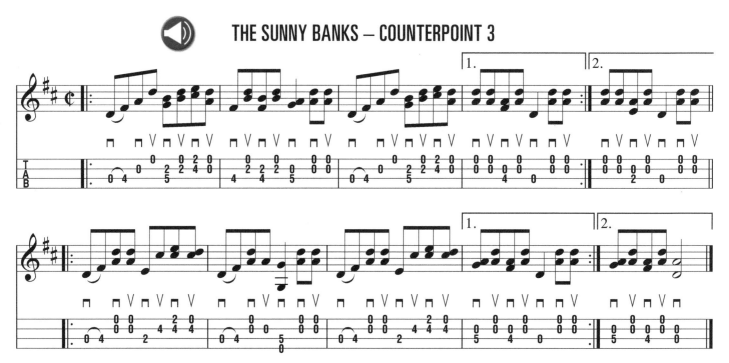

Listen to the next audio track to hear "The Sunny Banks" at a more typical session tempo.

THE SUNNY BANKS – AT TEMPO

THIRD TUNE: DROPS OF BRANDY

SLIP JIGS

A **slip jig** is similar to a double jig, with these exceptions:

- Whereas a double jig is in 6/8 with six eighth notes per measure, a slip jig is in **9/8** and has nine eighth notes per measure.

- While the double jig has its six eighth notes grouped into two groups of three with a two pulse, the slip jig has its nine eighth notes grouped in three groups of three with a *three* pulse.

We count slip jigs like this:

"**One** and uh, **Two** and uh, **Three** and uh."
1 2 3

Here is the melody to the popular slip jig, "Drops of Brandy." As with the double jig, a down-up-down picking pattern is best. Notice that the key signature now has one sharp—we are in the key of G major.

The melody is written and recorded here for your reference. Listen and get familiar with it, then learn the following accompaniment parts.

DROPS OF BRANDY – MELODY

DROPS OF BRANDY CHORDS

The first chord is a G5 chord. In this case, the only notes are G, D, D, and D (without the 3rd, or B, which would complete the major triad). This type of chord, often used in accompanying Irish traditional music, has the root (G) and 5th (D) played on all four courses at once to give a much fatter sound than a simple single-note drone.

Notice that the other chords, C and D, are only partially realized on the second and third courses while the low G and high D strings continue to be played open, providing a "G" drone over the changing chords. This is called a **suspension** (like the Asus4 chord you encountered earlier), when one or more notes are continued after other notes change to make a new chord. While this can be dissonant, it is a passing dissonance that can add a lot of character to an accompaniment.

DROPS OF BRANDY – SIMPLE CHORDS 1

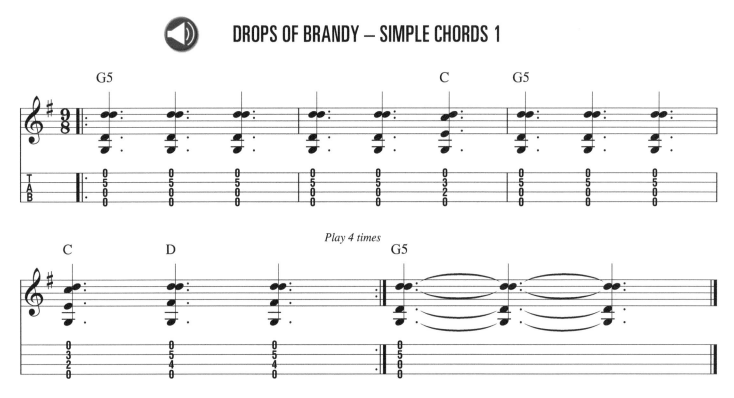

DROPS OF BRANDY ARPEGGIOS

In this example we have the same chords as in the last, but now we are playing them as arpeggios.

DROPS OF BRANDY – SIMPLE CHORDS 2

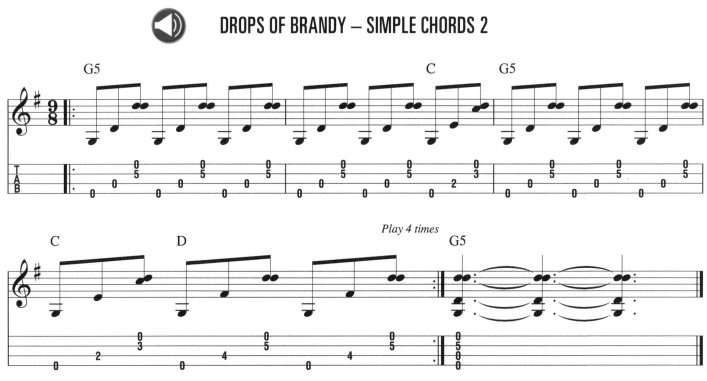

Now try this example, where we slightly alter the voicing of the chords.

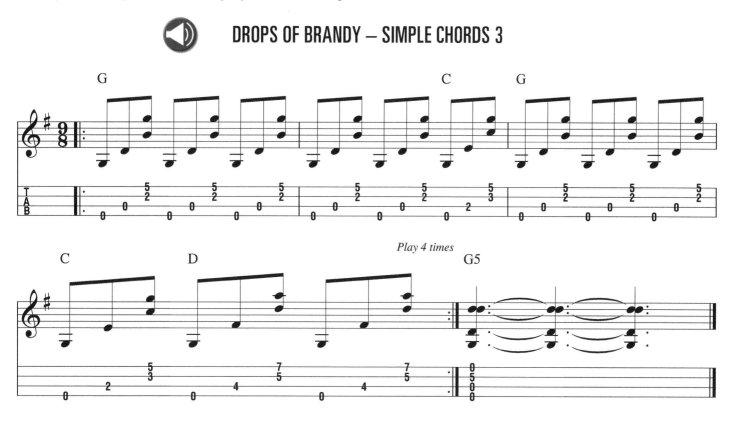

DROPS OF BRANDY – SIMPLE CHORDS 3

THE CAPO

The **capo** is a convenient way to change the pitch of the open strings of a fretted instrument without changing your tuning (which could endanger the instrument by varying the tension of the strings). When you clamp a capo on the neck across a certain fret, that fret becomes "open position." Most Irish bouzouki players use a capo and consider it an indispensable part of the instrument. Indeed, many of the sounds from the classic recordings would have been impossible without the capo.

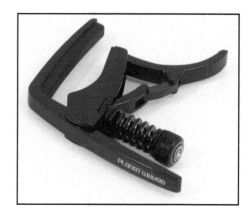

I recommend the type of capo that can be put on, taken off, or moved with only the fret hand. My favorite capo is the Planet Waves Tri-Action Capo. It has a spring so it can be moved or removed easily, but it also has a tension adjustment that allows you to set the tension just right for your instrument.

DROPS OF BRANDY COUNTERPOINT WITH ARPEGGIOS

Now we'll accompany the same tune, but instead of playing the G, C, and D chords in the open position, we'll add the capo at the fifth fret and use some of the D major harmonies from our first two tunes.

"Capo V" above the staff tells you to place the capo at fret 5. Line it up straight between the metal frets and put it closest to and just behind the 5th fret. Check your tuning after you put it on; sometimes a capo affects the instrument's intonation. Your "open" notes will now be (low to high): C–G–D–G.

Even though this tune is in G major, we are using D major fingerings and shapes because of the capo. If you are reading the tablature, you don't need to think about this difference once you have your capo on the fifth fret. The capoed fret will be "0" in tab (in this case, the 5th fret is "0"). If you are reading the notation, keep in mind that you will be "thinking" in D major even though everything you are playing is sounding in G major. This thinking in one key or mode while using the capo to actually play in another is a fundamental feature of the way the bouzouki is approached in Irish traditional music. The capo retains the essential drone nature of the open tuning but allows that sound to happen in more keys than D.

For reference, here is the "Drops of Brandy" melody again, this time arranged for capo V:

DROPS OF BRANDY – MELODY (CAPO V)

Capo V

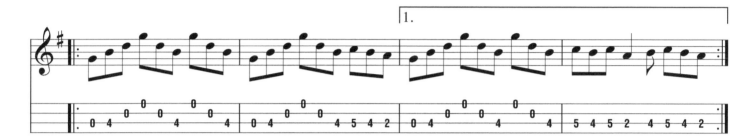

Now here's the first counterpoint accompaniment. Maintain the pick-hand pattern: down–up–down, down–up–down.

DROPS OF BRANDY – COUNTERPOINT 1

Capo V

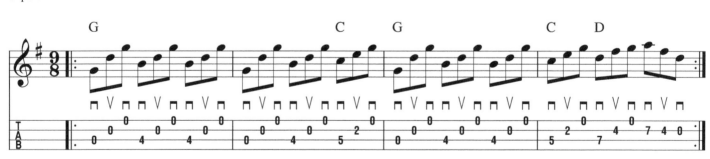

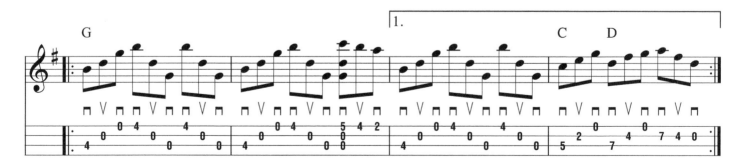

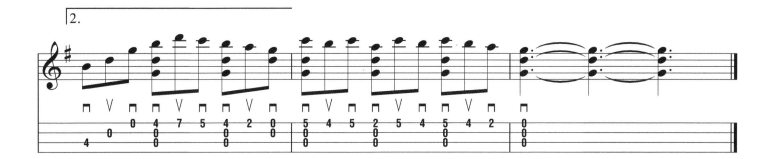

The next example includes some pull-offs. Remember to pluck the first note, then "pull off" your finger to make the second note sound without picking.

Pay particular attention to the pick-hand pattern in this one—there are a couple of differences from the previous example.

DROPS OF BRANDY — COUNTERPOINT 2

Capo V

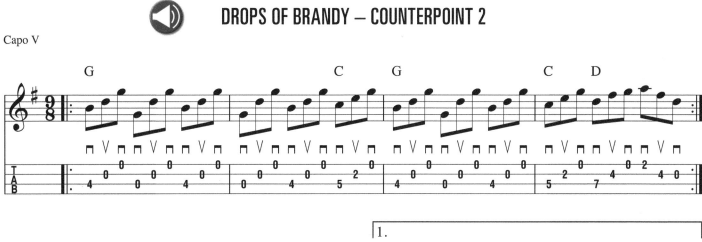

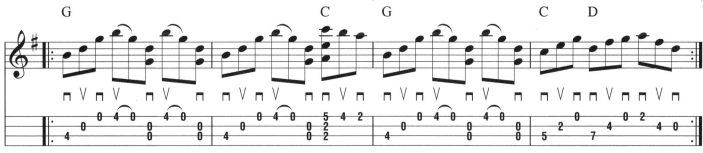

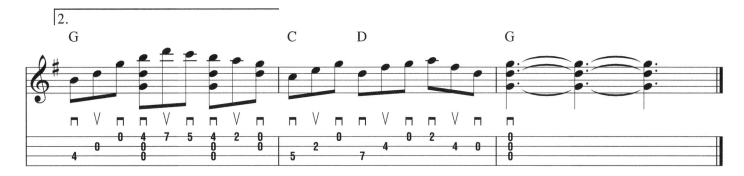

This example has more harmony notes and horizontal movement against the melody. Again, pay close attention to the pick-hand pattern as it has a few differences from the previous two examples.

 DROPS OF BRANDY – COUNTERPOINT 3

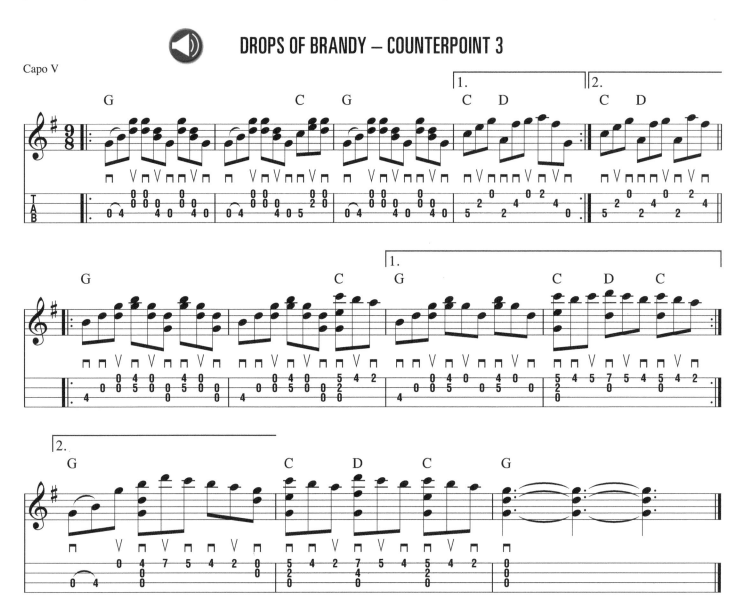

Here is the slip jig at a more typical session tempo with both melody and accompaniment.

 DROPS OF BRANDY – AT TEMPO

FOURTH TUNE: THE DUNMORE LASSES

"The Dunmore Lasses" is a standard reel in cut time with eight-measure parts (unlike "The Sunny Banks," which has four-measure parts). It sounds very good with the capo on the second fret, using D minor fingerings for this tune which is in E minor. The range of notes fits perfectly within five frets on the bouzouki, and the capo allows the open drone notes to ring in the key of E minor instead of D minor.

This melody, with its quick sixteenth notes, is here for your reference. Listen, read along, and get familiar with it; then learn the following accompaniment parts.

 THE DUNMORE LASSES – MELODY

Capo II

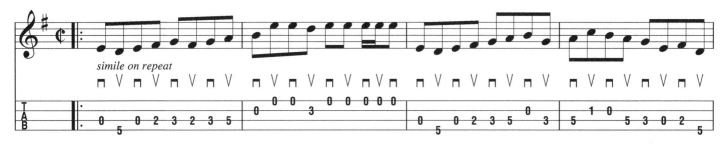

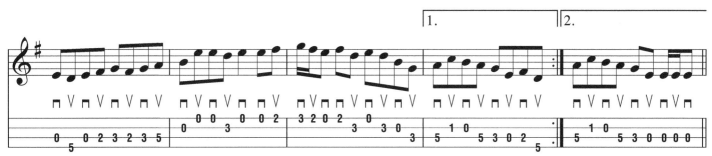

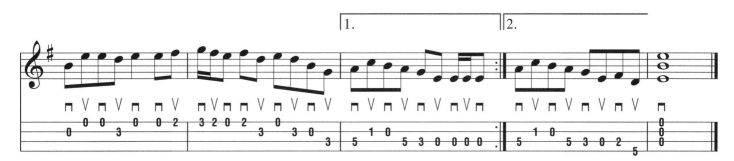

THE DUNMORE LASSES CHORDS

Here's a simple chordal accompaniment for "The Dunmore Lasses" that uses the capo on the second fret to allow a drone in E minor. Notice the repeated eighth notes on the high D course. Use the down-up picking pattern throughout.

Again, keep in mind that even though this tune is in E minor we are using D minor fingerings and shapes. Chord symbols reflect the actual sounding chords.

THE DUNMORE LASSES — CHORDS 1

Capo II

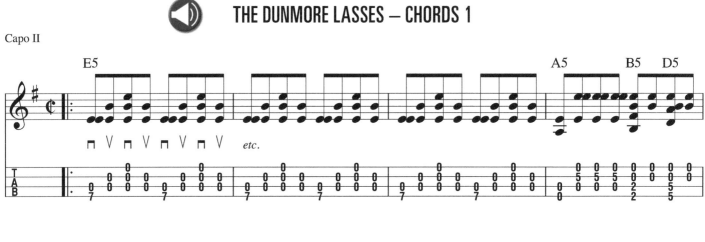

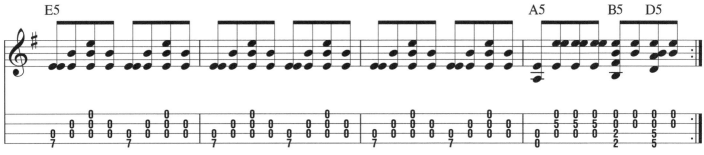

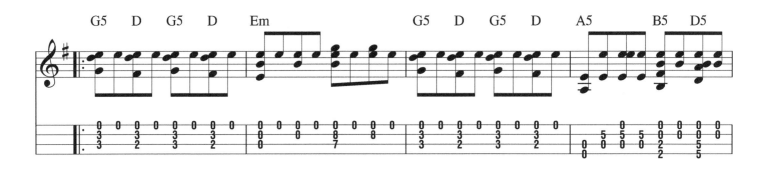

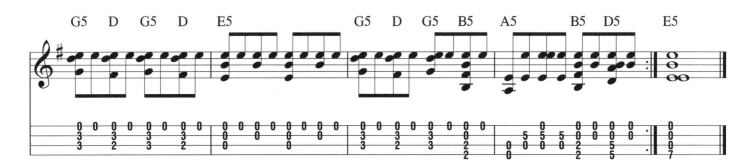

THE DUNMORE LASSES CHORDS AND COUNTERPOINT

Now we'll mix in a little more harmony and movement for a hybrid of the chordal and counterpoint approaches. The capo is still on fret 2.

THE DUNMORE LASSES – CHORDS 2

Here is the reel at a more typical session tempo with both melody and accompaniment.

THE DUNMORE LASSES – AT TEMPO

APPENDIX A: ACCOMPANIMENT IN IRISH TRADITIONAL MUSIC

The elements of accompaniment for Irish tunes are:

Rhythm—All accompaniment for dance music should have some percussive aspect. All bouzouki players, guitarists, or pianists would do well to listen extensively to master tune players, focusing on the rhythmic aspects of their playing.

Harmony—Creating counterpoint or chords that *complement* the melody. The art of accompaniment is the art of complementing a melody that someone else is playing. In Irish traditional music, accompaniments are usually improvised on the bouzouki, guitar, or piano. A skilled accompanist will know instantly whether a tune is a jig, reel, hornpipe, slide, or polka; what the key center is; and what mode the tune is in.

These skills come with years of practice and playing in sessions. Please be patient with yourself as you learn, and don't "bite off more than you can chew." Be sure you are ready for a next step before moving on. *Always* ask the more experienced players in your session for suggestions.

HARMONY IN TRADITIONAL IRISH MUSIC

"Chords," per se, are not really a part of the structure of Irish traditional music—at least not in the same way that chords are integral to bluegrass, blues, or rock 'n' roll. The harmony in Irish tunes is usually implied by the melody, and in some cases chords are completely spelled out in the form of arpeggios. Most of the time, the chords suggested by the melody are quite simple, but they are not necessarily obvious. For those who are new to the music, chords and chord changes in Irish music can be really tricky.

Chord "changes," such as the I–IV–I–V–IV–I of a 12-bar blues progression, are not really present. The chord changes in Irish tunes are usually just **cadences**—movements from one chord to another that have a satisfying sense of finality and are particular to each of the four modes (Ionian/major, Dorian, Mixolydian, Aeolian/minor) in which Irish music occurs.

A WORD ABOUT SESSIONS

Since about the middle of the last century, one of the native habitats for Irish traditional music has been the **session**, a musical gathering usually taking place in a pub. These days, sessions can be anywhere: bookstores, coffeehouses, music stores, etc.; but the setting is less important than the attitude with which the session is conducted. A session is a community event, much like an informal gathering of friends having a conversation over drinks. It is inclusive, or should be, but only to a point. Participation is not based simply on one's interest; one must be able to play the music to a reasonable minimum standard that is established by the regular players in that session. Many sessions, and most good ones, have a leader: an experienced player who can act more or less like a traffic cop, guiding the music-making, avoiding train wrecks, and arbitrating between competing egos if necessary. One thing to stress here: if you are interested in joining a session but are inexperienced, you really must talk to the session leader or the players who regularly anchor a session; let them know of your interest and willingness to learn. Most players, if approached in this way, will be helpful and encouraging. At the very least, you will avoid any faux pas or ruffling of feathers. And keep in mind that you will progress a lot faster and have more fun if you ask for guidance.

APPENDIX B: SUGGESTED LISTENING

Artist/Player	Title	Year	Label
J. Moynihan/ Andy Irvine	*Sweeney's Men*	1968	Transatlantic
J. Moynihan/ Andy Irvine	*The Tracks of Sweeney*	1969	Transatlantic
Planxty (Irvine/Lunny)	*Planxty*	1973	Shanachie 79009
Planxty (Irvine/Lunny)	*The Well Below the Valley*	1973	Shanachie 79010
Planxty (Irvine/Moynihan/Lunny)	*Cold Blow and the Rainy Night*	1974	Shanachie 79011
Matt Molloy with Dónal Lunny	*Matt Molloy*	1976	Compass LUN3004
Andy Irvine & Paul Brady	*Andy Irvine & Paul Brady*	1976	Compass LUN3008
Frankie Gavin & Alec Finn	*Traditional Music of Ireland*	1977	Shanachie 34009
Martin O'Connor w/ Dónal Lunny	*The Connaughtman's Rambles*	1979	Compass LUN3027
Mary Bergin with Alec Finn	*Féadoga Stain*	1979	Shanachie 79006
Planxty (Irvine/Lunny)	*After the Break*	1979	Tara
Planxty (Irvine/Lunny)	*The Woman I Loved So Well*	1980	Tara
De Dannan (Alec Finn)	*De Dannan*	1975	Polydor
Frank Harte with Dónal Lunny	*And Listen to My Song*	1975	Mulligan
The Bothy Band (Dónal Lunny)	*1975*	1975	Compass LUN3002
The Bothy Band (Dónal Lunny)	*Old Hag You Have Killed Me*	1976	Compass LUN3007
The Bothy Band (Dónal Lunny)	*Out of the Wind, Into the Sun*	1977	Compass LUN3013
The Bothy Band (Dónal Lunny)	*Afterhours*	1979	Compass LUN3030
De Dannan (Alec Finn)	*Selected Jigs, Reels & Songs*	1978	Decca
De Dannan (Alec Finn)	*The Star-Spangled Molly*	1978	Shanachie
De Dannan (Alec Finn)	*The Mist Covered Mountain*	1980	Gael Linn
Roger Landes	*Dragon Reels*	1997	Ranger RMCD 4321
Randal Bays & Roger Landes	*House to House*	2004	Foxglove FG0350

Also look for any recordings by the band Dervish: Michael Holmes (bouzouki) and Brian McDonagh (mandola).

Check out Andy Irvine's work with the band Patrick Street, as well as Andy's and Dónal Lunny's work with the band Mozaik.

ONLINE RESOURCES

YouTube has many excellent historical videos that are not only very entertaining but also worthy of study.

Search for "Andy Irvine," "Dónal Lunny," "Planxty," "Alec Finn," "De Dannan," "Dervish," and other names on the list above.

Learn To Play Today
with folk music instruction
from Hal Leonard

Hal Leonard Banjo Method – Second Edition

Authored by Mac Robertson, Robbie Clement & Will Schmid. This innovative method teaches 5-string, bluegrass style. The method consists of two instruction books and two cross-referenced supplement books that offer the beginner a carefully-paced and interest-keeping approach to the bluegrass style.

00699500	Book 1 Only	$7.99
00695101	Book 1 with Online Audio	$16.99
00699502	Book 2 Only	$7.99
00696056	Book 2 with CD	$16.9

Hal Leonard Brazilian Guitar Method

by Carlos Arana

This book uses popular Brazilian songs to teach you the basics of the Brazilian guitar style and technique. Learn to play in the styles of Joao Gilberto, Luiz Bonfá, Baden Powell, Dino Sete Cordas, Joao Basco, and many others! Includes 33 demonstration tracks.

00697415 Book/Online Audio $14.99

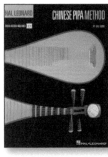

Hal Leonard Chinese Pipa Method

by Gao Hong

This easy-to-use book serves as an introduction to the Chinese pipa and its techniques. Lessons include: tuning • Western & Chinese notation basics • left and right hand techniques • positions • tremolo • bending • vibrato and overtones • classical pipa repertoire • popular Chinese folk tunes • and more!

00121398 Book/Online Video $19.99

Hal Leonard Dulcimer Method – Second Edition

by Neal Hellman

A beginning method for the Appalachian dulcimer with a unique new approach to solo melody and chord playing. Includes tuning, modes and many beautiful folk songs all demonstrated on the audio accompaniment. Music and tablature.

00699289	Book	$10.99
00697230	Book/Online Audio	$16.99

Hal Leonard Flamenco Guitar Method

by Hugh Burns

Traditional Spanish flamenco song forms and classical pieces are used to teach you the basics of the style and technique in this book. Lessons cover: strumming, picking and percussive techniques • arpeggios • improvisation • fingernail tips • capos • and much more. Includes flamenco history and a glossary.

00697363 Book/Online Audio $15.99

Hal Leonard Irish Bouzouki Method

by Roger Landes

This comprehensive method focuses on teaching the basics of the instrument as well as accompaniment techniques for a variety of Irish song forms. It covers: playing position • tuning • picking & strumming patterns • learning the fretboard • accompaniment styles • double jigs, slip jigs & reels • drones • counterpoint • arpeggios • playing with a capo • traditional Irish songs • and more.

00696348 Book/Online Audio $10.99

Hal Leonard Mandolin Method – Second Edition

Noted mandolinist and teacher Rich Del Grosso has authored this excellent mandolin method that features great playable tunes in several styles (bluegrass, country, folk, blues) in standard music notation and tablature. The audio features play-along duets.

00699296	Book	$7.99
00695102	Book/Online Audio	$15.99

Hal Leonard Oud Method

by John Bilezikjian

This book teaches the fundamentals of standard Western music notation in the context of oud playing. It also covers: types of ouds, tuning the oud, playing position, how to string the oud, scales, chords, arpeggios, tremolo technique, studies and exercises, songs and rhythms from Armenia and the Middle East, and 25 audio tracks for demonstration and play along.

00695836 Book/Online Audio $12.99

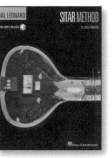

Hal Leonard Sitar Method

by Josh Feinberg

This beginner's guide serves as an introduction to sitar and its technique, as well as the practice, theory, and history of raga music. Lessons include: tuning • postures • right- and left-hand technique • Indian notation • raga forms; melodic patterns • bending strings • hammer-ons, pull-offs, and slides • changing strings • and more!

00696613	Book/Online Audio	$14.99
00198245	Book/Online Media	$19.99

Hal Leonard Ukulele Method

by Lil' Rev

This comprehensive and easy-to-use beginner's guide by acclaimed performer and uke master Lil' Rev includes many fun songs of different styles to learn and play. Includes: types of ukuleles, tuning, music reading, melody playing, chords, strumming, scales, tremolo, music notation and tablature, a variety of music styles, ukulele history and much more.

00695847	Book 1 Only	$6.99
00695832	Book 1 with Online Audio	$10.99
00695948	Book 2 Only	$6.99
00695949	Book 2 with Online Audio	$10.99

Visit Hal Leonard Online at
www.halleonard.com

Prices and availability subject to change without notice.